A 30-Day Prayer Journey

Isaiah T. Hayes

ISBN 979-8-89526-221-4 (paperback)
ISBN 979-8-89526-222-1 (digital)

Copyright © 2024 by Isaiah T. Hayes

All rights reserved. No part of this publication may be reproduced, distributed, or transmitted in any form or by any means, including photocopying, recording, or other electronic or mechanical methods without the prior written permission of the publisher. For permission requests, solicit the publisher via the address below.

Christian Faith Publishing
832 Park Avenue
Meadville, PA 16335
www.christianfaithpublishing.com

Printed in the United States of America

Day 1 of 30 Prayer for Wives

Thought: How has your wife made you a better man?

Scripture: "Whoso findeth a wife findeth a good thing, and obtaineth favour of the Lord" (Proverbs 18:22 KJV).

Husbands, Remember Your Good Thing!

As many of us have experienced in our marriage, it's easy to get frustrated, upset, and project the day's battles onto our wives. But remember that God has deemed our wives *our good thing*! Our wives are the backbones of the family; they are the foundation that holds us up when we are ready to crumble. Our wives have matured us from bachelors chasing women into men who desired to become husbands, providing a life for a woman we couldn't imagine living without, from husbands into fathers (future fathers), and turning our houses into homes. We have truly been blessed with women that *we can call our good thing*!

Prayer for wives: Lord, let us, as husbands, never forsake or take for granted *our good thing*. We pray a special blessing over the women who have inspired us to become better men each and every day. In Jesus's name, Amen!

Day 2 of 30 Prayer for Wives

Thought: What if she said, "No"?

Scripture: "Husbands, love your wives, even as Christ also loved the church, and gave himself for it" (Ephesians 5:25 KJV).

Husbands, Remember the Trust Factor!

We sometimes forget that our wives could've said, "No!" Man, what a game-changer that would've been, right? But she *trusted* you with her "yes." Not only did she trust you, her parents, you *trusted you*, and most importantly, *God*.

At many wedding ceremonies, the presiding official will ask, "Who gives this woman to this man?" The response is normally, "I do," or "We do." You see, this "I do" means more than, "Take care of my baby." It symbolizes that "I do trust you to provide a better life, I do trust you to give her a love that lasts a lifetime, I do trust you that you will make her a better woman, I do trust you that you will be able to provide her with things that I or we could've only dreamed of, I do trust that you will exhaust every avenue to do what you need to do as a husband to make it happen. I do! Then God asks this of us as husbands: "Love your wives as Christ loved the church." Are you willing to give your life for your good thing, boo thang, ride-or-die, your lover, and your best friend? Are you willing to fight with everything in you to love your wife as Christ loved the church? This may mean losing relationships with close friends and loved ones, sacrificing time, resources, and efforts to accommodate and provide for her. At the end of the day, you are a highly *trusted* individual. She *trusted you, her parents trusted you, God trusted you*, but they all still trusted you with, "I do"!

Prayer: God, thank you for trusting us as husbands with one of the most precious gifts life has to offer. We ask that as you and many others continue to trust us that we will evolve into husbands that we never knew existed, that we will be husbands who love our wives as you loved the church. In Jesus's name, Amen!

Day 3 of 30 Prayer for Wives

Thought: What is a king without his crown?

Scripture: "A worthy wife is a crown for her husband, but a disgraceful woman is like cancer in his bones" (Proverbs 12:4 NLT).

An Indispensable Crown

A *worthy wife* is a crown for her husband! A crown is one of the most recognized pieces of attire concerning a king, but what king walks around without his crown? A king takes pride in how the crown makes him feel, look, and what it symbolizes. How do our wives make us feel, look, and what do they symbolize in our lives? Scripture reminds us that they should be *our crown* if she is worthy. A crown isn't something we should allow to collect dust or pull out for special occasions; it is to be worn every day with a sense of pride and honor. When thinking of our wives, we should begin to think of a king's crown and how indispensable it really is, and that our wives hold a priceless value in our lives. How will you wear your "crown" today?

Prayer: God, thank you for adorning us with precious women who are the crowns we wear every day. We ask that we never devalue the significance it means to wake up each and every day next to them. Our wives have given us an added value that we could not afford ourselves, so continue to bless our queens in every endeavor, so that we may see your glory rest on their lives. I ask that you help us become greater husbands with each passing day. In Jesus's name. Amen!

Day 4 of 30 Prayer for Wives

Thought: Do you handle situations on your job with the same care as in your home?

Scripture: "Husbands, love your wives, and be not bitter against them" (Colossians 3:19 KJV).

Fragile…Handle with Care!

It's amazing how our lovely wives can bring us so much joy and then *boom*…they can become a thorn in our side. The same women we would give our lives for in an instant are the same women we can't understand at times. It's frustrating being a husband sometimes and, rightfully so, trying to figure out what our wives really mean or need from us. I believe most of us have experienced the situation of "I need you to spend more time with me," then you're hit with "We're around each other *all day, every day*, and I just need time to myself." Look, it happens, but instead of getting frustrated or allowing the bitter words to fly, take a moment to reflect on situations that have transpired at work, church, in the classroom, and/or dealing with clients. How did you handle those situations? Did you become bitter and say things that put your job in jeopardy? Probably not!

So why do we not realize that every time we say something sharp, harsh, nasty, mean, and out of frustration, we can lose the love of our lives? I'm not saying they will ask for a divorce, but we are slowly pushing them away. No matter how long we have been married, we'll always learn something new about our wives as time passes. We have the opportunity to love our wives in those moments and handle the situation as a package labeled: Fragile…Handle with Care! Will you break your wife, or will you handle her with care?

Prayer: God, you know how lovely our wives are and how they can be very difficult to understand from time to time, but we ask you for your wisdom that will allow us to handle them with care in situations that could very well break them. Allow us to become husbands who ask questions when we don't fully understand what is being asked of us, and more importantly, let us become husbands who are swift to hear, slow to speak, and slow to wrath. In Jesus's name. Amen!

Day 5 of 30 Prayer for Wives

Thought: Are you living up to your *full* potential as a husband?

Scripture: "In the same way, you husbands must give honor to your wives. Treat your wife with understanding as you live together. She may be weaker than you are, but she is your equal partner in God's gift of new life. Treat her as you should so your prayers will not be hindered" (1 Peter 3:7 NLT).

Your Actions Hinder Your Prayers!

When reading this passage of Scripture, it tells us that the wife is the "weaker vessel," but how we interpret that has a direct impact on our prayers. Let's be honest for a minute: How many times has your wife given you advice, and you heard her but failed to *listen to her*? Truth be told, she is right 9 out of 10 times. Let us not be quick to mistake "weak" for a lack of wisdom, experience, and understanding.

If we take an honest look at this, how many times have we been the "weaker vessel"? I mean *weaker* as the inability to communicate effectively with our wives without wearing our hearts or frustrations on our sleeves? The inability to see that she hurts just as we hurt? The inability to realize that she is stronger than us in many situations? When we become the "weaker vessels" due to our inability to see, communicate, and show compassion, this has and will continue to hinder our prayers. Always keep in mind that our wives will *never forget* (1) what we did to make them feel unappreciated, and (2) what we have said to make them feel devalued. Let us live up to the *full potential* God intended for us to be as husbands by treating our wives with honor, respect, love, understanding, tenderness, and patience.

Prayer: God, forgive me for being a less-than-adequate husband more times than not. Give us the wisdom as husbands to realize the way to effectively communicate and love our wives without all the extra. Allow us to become husbands who are strong where our wives are weak, and allow our wives to be strong where we are weak. We desire our marriage to be as strong as it has ever been. Keep us, lead us, and help us from hindering our prayers by our actions. In Jesus's name, Amen!

Day 6 of 30 Prayer for Wives

Thought: Is your marriage 50:50, 80:20, 99:1, or 100:100?

Scripture: "As the Scriptures say, 'A man leaves his father and mother and is joined to his wife, and the two are united into one.' This is a great mystery, but it is an illustration of the way Christ and the church are one" (Ephesians 5:31–32 NLT).

You + Your Wife = One

When has one plus one ever equaled one? Never! But in marriage, math is done a little differently. You see, most people believe marriage is 50:50, but in reality, we should never encounter a day where a full 100 percent effort isn't given on our part. The same effort put forth to get your wife should be the same to keep her. Husbands, let's not forget our debonair ways: the opening of car doors, pulling chairs out, writing letters, wearing her favorite cologne, and sending flowers. Pouring out a love that you would want to be a recipient of in your marriage doesn't make you weak; it makes you human. Now, becoming one will take time and include a lifetime of patience, understanding, effort, communication, and prayer, among other things. Always remember, when things get difficult, ask yourself this question: Will this benefit me or our marriage?

Prayer: God, help us to yearn for a willingness to become one with the love of our life. We ask that your divine wisdom would lead and guide us in every area of our marriage. We ask that, as we continue to pray for our wives, we will become sensitive to their needs and set the bar to another level as husbands. We thank you for all things. In Jesus's name, Amen!

Day 7 of 30 Prayer for Wives

Thought: What makes you a good husband?
Scripture: "Let no one split apart what God has joined together" (Mark 10:9 NLT).

Outside Interference

We all have that one childhood friend, coworker, or family member who is single and is always trying to get you to relive your college days, premarital days, or, better yet, telling you how to stay married. It's easy to get caught up in the advice of family and friends and begin to lose ourselves in how others have managed their marriages for years. As we all know, every marriage is different and every wife is very unique, but isn't it something how people who have been married for years can just fall out of love? I don't believe anyone can fall out of love overnight. However, I do believe that outside influences over a period of time play a very important role (women who will listen to your problems, friends encouraging your frustrations, and family members influencing thoughts of you becoming single again). All these things interfere with our love for our wives and ultimately cause us to reconsider marriage. Outside interference only benefits one party. What I want us to ponder as husbands is this: If our wives had those influences, how would it make us feel?

Prayer: God, help us as husbands to acknowledge outside interferences and influences that are detrimental and determined to ruin our marriage and the love we possess for our wives. Allow us to come to you openly, honestly, and faithfully, to allow your divine wisdom to push us to become more faithful than we've ever been. Give us eyes, hearts, and souls only for our wives. We thank you in advance for your divine intervention on our behalf. In Jesus's name, Amen!

Day 8 of 30 Prayer for Wives

Thought: Don't allow your blessing to become your burden!

Scripture: "Love never gives up, never loses faith, is always hopeful, and endures through every circumstance" (1 Corinthians 13:7 NLT).

A Will to Fight

A wife is one of our greatest blessings, and at times, she can feel like one of our greatest burdens. We may encounter times when throwing in the towel seems like the best and only option. We are reminded in this scripture that love *never loses faith* (faith is the substance of things hoped for and the evidence of things not yet seen) and endures through every circumstance—*every circumstance*! Stay hopeful even when things are the worst they have ever been, and remember the reason why you prayed for a wife.

Remember why you fell in love with her, the reason why God blessed you with her, and the reason why you overcame the obstacles to stay and fight for your marriage. God blessed you with your bride to help you, bless you, and love you! Every marriage runs into difficult times, and in those times, love, endure, pray, and fight like hell to keep the blessing of God in the form of your bride.

Prayer: God, give us an enduring love for our wives—love that matures us as husbands and exemplifies the patience of Christ. Allow us to pray in moments of frustration and misunderstandings, and continue to fight every day to prevent our blessing, our wife, from becoming a burden. In Jesus's name, Amen!

Day 9 of 30 Prayer for Wives

Thought: If you could change one thing about you, what would it be?

Scripture: "Love is patient and kind. Love is not jealous or boastful or proud or rude. It does not demand its own way. It is not irritable, and it keeps no record of being wronged" (1 Corinthians 13:4–5 NLT).

Who Is Winning?

Do you count wins and losses? Rights and wrongs? Good times and bad? It's easy to get caught up in a competitive nature and relive our "glory days," but keeping track of how and when we win and are wronged in marriage is not recommended. A reoccurring thought for our marriages should be: Love is patient, kind, and not rude, proud, jealous or boastful! Let's be honest: If we allow the latter characteristics to entangle themselves in our marriage, we lose. More importantly, our marriage will lose. What if we did boast about our wives every day? How would that make them feel? What if we talked about how beautiful, smart, kind, understanding, and loving our wives were on a daily basis? Would we realize how blessed we truly are? Fellas, if you haven't realized it by now, you are *winning*! You won the day you tied the knot with your bride. You won when she gave you her heart, and you will continue to win if you apply all the characteristics of love in your marriage on a daily basis.

Prayer: God, thank you for this opportunity to continue to pray for our wives and the ability to become better husbands daily. Continue to show us the areas we need improvement in making our marriage the best that it can be. In Jesus's name, Amen!

Day 10 of 30 Prayer for Wives

Thought: What is the last spontaneous thing you have done for your wife?

Scripture: "Then the Lord God said, 'It is not good for the man to be alone. I will make a helper who is just right for him'" (Genesis 2:18 NLT).

You Got the Right One!

She's your yin to your yang, ride or die, love of your life, mother to your children, and the best thing that has happened to you. Let's take a moment and *thank God* for taking the time to create your wife just for you. We've all had thoughts of the ideal woman, what she would look like, smell like, and what we would say to her, but plans changed as your future wife walked through those doors. How is it that God thought enough of us to create such a beautiful person? A woman who is meant to help us and who is *just right for us*! A woman that is *just right for you was created by God with you in mind*! Here's the secret: She's here to help you! Some call our wives a helpmeet, and in all honesty, that's true. Wives help us meet our toughest challenges, goals, dreams, and aspirations and help us overcome shortcomings, hurts, pains, and greatest fears with unmatched confidence. Our wives have made us better men, husbands, fathers, teachers, and lovers. Let's not be too quick to tune out their advice. Keep in mind she's meant to *help*, not hurt you!

Prayer: God, thank you for thinking enough of us to send us a helpmeet—the women who have shaped us from good men into great husbands, fathers, and providers. Thank you for giving us exactly what we needed to help us in this journey of life, and let us not forsake the help you have sent us. Thank you! In Jesus's name, Amen!

Day 11 of 30 Prayer for Wives

Thought: When was the last time you encouraged your wife to pursue her dreams?

Scripture: "So the Lord God caused the man to fall into a deep sleep. While the man slept, the Lord God took out one of the man's ribs and closed up the opening. Then the Lord God made a woman from the rib, and he brought her to the man. 'At last!' the man exclaimed. 'This one is bone from my bone and flesh from my flesh! She will be called "woman" because she was taken from "man."'" (Genesis 2:21–23 NLT).

Your Rib

Can you imagine the excitement Adam was feeling? The relief? *After all this time, I finally have someone that was made from me for me! At last!* Do you ever have those "at last" moments in your marriage?

The moments that you can't wait for your wife to get home so the kids can calm down, help with homework, or just so you can hear about her day?

Adam was well aware of what Eve's purpose in his life was as his wife, but do we? Do we get excited when we walk through the doors and our wives are there to greet us, love on us, and make sure dinner is prepared and the house is clean after they have worked a full day too? Or do we fail to acknowledge it? When your wife took your last name, she took on the responsibility of her purpose in your life, your children's, as well as fulfilling her own as a wife, woman, and mother. See, God took a rib and created something we couldn't live without, and Adam's comment of "at last" is proof of it.

Prayer: God, thank you! Thank you for our wives and the purpose that they will fulfill in our lives. My prayer is that you would allow us as husbands to fulfill our purpose in their lives by being their "at last." Keep us with a spirit of humility and humbleness to love our wives with such passion, compassion, patience, understanding, and gentleness that we begin to lose ourselves in the love you have ordained for our marriages. Thank you in advance, in Jesus's name, Amen!

Day 12 of 30 Prayer for Wives

Thought: How would life be without your wife?
Scripture: "Love each other with genuine affection, and take delight in honoring each other" (Romans 12:10 NLT).

Be Intentional

Take a moment and think about how you have become a better man since your wife has come into your life. Now take a moment and imagine if she were no longer in your life. Some of us can't even fix our minds to imagine what life would be like without our wives. What if we cherished our wives as if we were to lose them tomorrow? How would that shape our marriages?

If we are to become better husbands, let's cherish every moment that we are privileged to spend with our wives. Let's love them as if it were our last time and without any regrets. Take time to tell your wives how much they mean to you, how much you appreciate them, how much you love them, and how they have helped you become a better man. Let's become intentional in the ways we express our appreciation for our wives.

Prayer: God, allow us not to take for granted the opportunities we have to love and appreciate our wives. Continue to bless us with the wisdom to express our love in a meaningful and healthy way. We thank you and bless you in Jesus's name, Amen!

Day 13 of 30 Prayer for Wives

Thought: Are you holding true to your vows?

Scripture: "Always be humble and gentle. Be patient with each other, making allowance for each other's faults because of your love" (Ephesians 4:2 NLT).

How Deep Is Your Love?

We're human, and we all make mistakes, but do we hold onto some mistakes longer than others? Do we remind our wives of the mistakes they have made? Do we remind ourselves of the mistakes we have made? This scripture reminds us again of the patience that we should have with one another, but more importantly concerning each other's faults because of your love!

Do you love your wife more than her mistakes, shortcomings, and flaws? Or do you point out everything that is wrong with her every chance you get? How deep does your love truly run for your wife?

Prayer: God, thank you for pointing out the things that have hindered us as husbands. Allow us to give our wives the same patience that we give ourselves when our own faults come into play. Thank you for allowing us to grow daily as husbands in love, patience, compassion, and understanding of our wives and their needs with each passing day. In Jesus's name, Amen!

Day 14 of 30 Prayer for Wives

Thought: What sacrifices have you made lately for your marriage?

Scripture: "Who can find a virtuous and capable wife? She is more precious than rubies. Her husband can trust her, and she will greatly enrich his life. She brings him good, not harm, all the days of her life" (Proverbs 31:10–12 NLT).

Being Married Is Priceless

Who knew the benefits that a wife brought to the table? She greatly *enriches our lives*! She brings *good, not harm, all the days of her life*! If we were aware of the favor that accompanied our wives, we might have married sooner. If you knew then what you know now, how would that have shaped you as a husband? Now, knowing what you know about marriage, how will you apply it moving forward? Will you be able to bring good and not harm to your wife for the rest of your days? Will you ensure that she is valued more than precious rubies? Let's be better husbands today than we were yesterday!

Prayer: God, thank you for peeling back the layers that have prevented us from seeing our wives for their true value. Allow us to treat them and see them with your eyes and love them with your heart. In Jesus's name, Amen!

Day 15 of 30 Prayer for Wives

Thought: What areas of concern in your marriage have you asked God to help you in?

Scripture: "Three things will last forever—faith, hope, and love—and the greatest of these is love" (1 Corinthians 13:13 NLT).

Marriage Is Honorable

Do you view your marriage as an honorable thing? God does! You have the honor of calling the love of your life your wife! Think about this for a minute—being introduced as the honorable husband! The husband who's always going above and beyond the call of duty, loving in unlovable situations, and remaining composed in high-stress situations. Now, as husbands, does that sound like our wives? Going above the call of duty, loving in unlovable situations, and remaining composed in high-stress situations. The honorable wife is a woman who is able to handle any personality, seamlessly dealing with us as husbands, our children, their jobs, and monthly situations that we wouldn't even wish on any other human, but she is always giving more of herself than asked. If you ask me, I would say that is a very honorable thing.

Prayer: God, thank you for making marriage an honorable thing. We thank you for giving us the honor to wake up to beautiful wives. Allow us to never forget how honorable our marriages are in your sight. In Jesus's name, Amen!

Day 16 of 30 Prayer for Wives

Thought: How much does your wife mean to you?

Scripture: "In the same way, husbands ought to love their wives as they love their own bodies. For a man who loves his wife actually shows love for himself" (Ephesians 5:28 NLT).

Love Does a Body Good

How much do you love your body? Do you work out, eat healthy, and make sure it's in the best shape possible? Do you invest the same amount of time and effort in your marriage as you do in your body? We ought to love our wives as our own bodies. When was the last time you checked to see if your effort for a healthy body matched a healthy marriage? Let's not put more time in the gym working out than creating a healthier marriage.

Prayer: God, the same intent we use at the gym to ensure a better body and healthier lifestyle, allow us as husbands to put forth that same effort, intensity, drive, blood, sweat, and tears into our wives. I thank you in advance. In Jesus's name, Amen!

Day 17 of 30 Prayer for Wives

Thought: What are you doing to grow in marriage on a daily basis?

Scripture: "And do everything with love" (1 Corinthians 16:14 NLT).

More than Just a Word

Marriage is a unique recipe that requires patience, compassion, wisdom, and, most importantly, a great deal of love. Love is a powerful word, but it also requires action. Is your marriage lacking any key ingredients? If so, you have probably cut back on your love. As I'm learning, *love* brings the perfect balance to a marriage. What type of compassion can one have without love? What type of patience can one have without love? What type of wisdom can one give without love? It is love that ties all these ingredients together to make a great marriage work. When times get rough in marriage, sprinkle love on compassion, wisdom, understanding, and patience wherever it is needed most to ensure that your marriage is the best that it can be.

Prayer: God, bless us to love in everything that we do in our marriage. Give us wisdom in difficult times that points to love and not hurt. You know where we fall short in our marriages, and we ask that you would sprinkle some additional love, wisdom, compassion, or whatever you see we need most in our marriage to make it not only great but blessed. In Jesus's name, Amen!

Day 18 of 30 Prayer for Wives

Thought: When is the last time you and your wife prayed or fasted together?

Scripture: "Do not deprive each other of sexual relations, unless you both agree to refrain from sexual intimacy for a limited time so you can give yourselves more completely to prayer. Afterward, you should come together again so that Satan won't be able to tempt you because of your lack of self-control" (1 Corinthians 7:5 NLT).

Spiritually Intimate

I don't know how many men have ever used the excuse of being mad at their wives to forgo sexual intimacy, but I'm guessing not many. If we are to refrain from sexual intimacy, it should be for the sole purpose of drawing closer to God as a couple. Let me ask you this: Did you pray with your wife this morning? Did you both tell God the things you need him to do for your marriage? What about for your children? What about your financial situation? In marriage, we run into many of the issues named above, but are you getting God's attention? When we realize that God isn't a genie to be called on in certain situations in marriage but in *all situations*, then we will begin to see God move like never before in our marriages. Let's be intentional with our intimate time with God and watch your marriage flourish.

Prayer: God, allow us to schedule time to pray and fast with our wives to get into your presence. Allow us to be transparent and sincere in seeking your face in our marriage by taking the time to abstain from sexual intimacy and become spiritually intimate with you. Bless us as only you can, in Jesus's name, Amen!

Day 19 of 30 Prayer for Wives

Thought: As a husband, what is your wife's greatest desire?

Scripture: "But Ruth replied, 'Don't ask me to leave you and turn back. Wherever you go, I will go; wherever you live, I will live. Your people will be my people, and your God will be my God. Wherever you die, I will die, and there I will be buried. May the Lord punish me severely if I allow anything but death to separate us!'" (Ruth 1:16–17 NLT).

Ride-or-Die Type of Love

What if our wives' greatest desire is more than us washing dishes, folding clothes, cleaning up after ourselves, loving on them, and taking time to listen more? Do you know? Have you asked? All jokes aside, what if your wife's greatest desire is as strong as Ruth's sentiments in this passage? Is that love too much? Will it push you away? Did you marry just for companionship (the fear of not being alone), or did you marry to share the rest of your life with this woman, to build a legacy, and to leave an inheritance to your children and grandchildren? Are you able, as a husband, to meet her greatest need? Take time this week and find out what your wife's greatest desire is, and you might be surprised.

Prayer: God, allow us to meet our wives' greatest needs and desires by losing ourselves in heart-to-heart conversations, doing more listening than talking, and more praying than assuming. Give us divine wisdom to apply the things in our marriages that are expressed. Bless us with the patience to properly apply these things in our marriages. In Jesus's name, Amen!

Day 20 of 30 Prayer for Wives

Thought: Have you asked God to make you the husband he desires you to be lately?

Scripture: "Trust in the Lord with all your heart; do not depend on your own understanding" (Proverbs 3:5 NLT).

Bragging Rights

Have you ever felt that you were a great husband? Has God ever shown you differently? It's easy to get caught up in the hype of thinking you're a good husband, especially if your wife's friends always say, "I wish my husband was a good man like yours." Honestly, every marriage is different, and as the saying goes, "Everything that glitters ain't gold." The scripture tells us not to lean on our own understanding, and it's simply for our own benefit. Have you ever known you were right about a thing and then, *boom*, found out you were wrong? Our way isn't the best way, but God's way will always take you to a place of greater understanding. Here is a thought: Are you content with just thinking, *I'm a good husband?* Or do you want to be a godly husband whose wife brags about how great a man, provider, comforter, and lover you are? Let's leave the bragging to God and our wives and continue as husbands to allow God's unchanging hand to bring glory and greater understanding to our marriages.

Prayer: God, forgive me for every time I thought I was a good husband but have fallen short of your expectations. Allow us as husbands to seek your face, wisdom, and guidance in becoming greater husbands with each passing day so that you may get the glory. Thank you for being patient with us and continuing to lead us as men wanting to fulfill this great call of being husbands. We bless your name. In Jesus's name, Amen!

Day 21 of 30 Prayer for Wives

Thought: As a husband, what would you consider to be your greatest strength and weakness in your marriage?

Scripture: "Two people are better off than one, for they can help each other succeed. If one person falls, the other can reach out and help. But someone who falls alone is in real trouble" (Ecclesiastes 4:9–10 NLT).

Support System

We live in a society where we will all need help at some point in life, and the best part for us as husbands is we have wives to keep us straight. Have you ever had a day when things were so bad that it took you out of character? Then your wife asks, "How was your day?" and just sits listening and calmly talking you off the ledge. We at times forget that our wives have saved us from heaps of trouble and bad decision-making. Our wives are praying for us, giving wisdom, encouraging us, loving us, and have been our biggest supporters.

What if we didn't have them to support us? Or encourage us or let us know that they are praying for us? What would be the success rate of the outcomes concerning bad days? This scripture tells us, "If you fall alone, you are in real trouble." See, our wives are stronger than society gives them credit for, and it goes beyond childbirth. They have the innate ability to keep us together when we have those moments of vulnerability. Our wives are the glue to many pieces in our lives when we have fallen, cracked, broken, and succumbed to the pressures of the world.

It's these strong women who have picked us up, dusted us off, and encouraged us to keep fighting for what we believe. So two are better than one, and our wives are more than deserving of the same actions in return. Let's make it a habit of encouraging, praying, and supporting them.

Prayer: God, thank you for blessing us with great wives who have been strong for us in our moments of weakness. Thank you for their strength, wisdom, confidence, compassion, understanding, and love, for without it, we would be lost. Allow us to give that same support to them as they have given to us. Allow us never to forget that the one who falls alone is in real trouble. I ask that you continue to lead and guide us in this lifelong journey and never allow us to fall alone, in Jesus's name, Amen!

Day 22 of 30 Prayer for Wives

Thought: If your wife lost her memory and forgot who you were, would you be willing to do the things to make her fall in love with you again?

Scripture: "Love does no wrong to others, so love fulfills the requirements of God's law" (Romans 13:10 NLT)

For Better or Worse

For better or worse, till death do you part! Does that sound familiar? Marriage is a lifelong commitment, and sometimes we don't understand the "for better or worse" until it happens. The "better"—the birth of a child, purchasing your first home, upgrading vehicles, taking nice vacations, and promotions on the job. We've all been there, and those moments are unforgettable. The "worse"—the moments when you lose a parent or a child, the threat of divorce, losing a job, losing a home, losing a car, and when your spouse falls gravely ill. Unfortunately, these are unforgettable moments also. However, it doesn't change the vow made before God, and it definitely shouldn't change your love for your wife. Or does it?

Our love should grow stronger with each passing day for our wives. No matter the circumstances or situations, we should try to perfect our love each and every day. Will it be tough at times? Yes, but you will be able to do it. Over the next few days, I challenge you to go back and do some of the things that you did when you first started dating your wife: leaving notes, sending flowers, going on a mini vacation, giving massages, and whatever comes to mind. Start rekindling a love in your marriage that won't go out regardless of any trial or situation that you may face.

Prayer: God, help us in times of stress and uncertainty to seek your face for guidance and wisdom concerning our marriages. I ask that you give us new and innovative ways to keep our marriages fresh and with a growing love for our wives. In Jesus's name, Amen!

Day 23 of 30 Prayer for Wives

Thought: What is one of your greatest moments in marriage?

Scripture: "Never let loyalty and kindness leave you! Tie them around your neck as a reminder. Write them deep within your heart. Then you will find favor with both God and people, and you will earn a good reputation" (Proverbs 3:3–4 NLT).

A Good Reputation

As a husband, doesn't it feel good hearing others talk about how good of a man you are? How does your reputation as a husband precede you? Is it one that reminds others of how thoughtful, compassionate, understanding, and loving you are? Or is it one that others can't stand to be in your presence?

The benefits of being loyal and kind are worth reaping. We will find *favor with God and people*, then we will earn a good reputation. The favor of God is unmerited; no matter what we do or say, we'll never be deserving of it, but it's amazing how God will still bestow it upon us. The favor of people will hold this statement true every time: "It's not what you know but who you know." This only reigns true if we keep loyalty and kindness in our hearts. Let's allow our reputations to precede us in finding favor with all we come in contact with and be more of a blessing in our marriages. *Favor will open doors that have been closed!*

Prayer: Thank you, God, for your favor and allowing us to obtain good reputations. We ask that we are able to find favor this week in every avenue of our lives, especially our marriages. Continue to keep and lead us into greater wisdom and patience concerning our wives. In Jesus's name, Amen!

Day 24 of 30 Prayer for Wives

Thought: Is it worth the argument?

Scripture: "And 'don't sin by letting anger control you.' Don't let the sun go down while you are still angry" (Ephesians 4:26 NLT).

No Room for Anger

How many times has your wife intentionally or unintentionally made you upset? Probably too many times to count, right? How many nights have you gone to sleep angry and woken up angry about the same thing from the day prior? Did you feel like an eye for an eye was the appropriate response? Or did you allow the anger to build up and then let your wife have it one unexpected day?

Anger is a tool used to bring you out of character and to do and say hurtful things. If we allow anger to control us, it will ultimately control our marriages, and we will fall victim to sin. Now sin doesn't mean adulterous relationships, but it could lead to them by allowing unforgiveness, hatred, bitterness, and lustful thinking to set in. How will you handle your next potential argument, debate, or heated conversation? Will it be with the wisdom of not responding until cooler heads prevail or by allowing anger to rear its head?

Prayer: God, sometimes we get extremely angry and say or do things that are hurtful and demeaning to our wives. We ask that you would help us in those moments of anger to remain silent or to walk away. We love our wives too much to kill them with our harsh words, but we need your help. Give us divine wisdom to be able to do so, allowing us to cut down those types of conversations to a minimum in our marriages. In Jesus's name, Amen!

Day 25 of 30 Prayer for Wives

Thought: Do you have positive influences that encourage your marriage?

Scripture: "Many waters cannot quench love, nor can rivers drown it. If a man tried to buy love with all his wealth, his offer would be utterly scorned" (Song of Songs 8:7 NLT).

This Love Is Not for Sale

How would you describe your love within your marriage? Would you be able to place a monetary value on it? We live in a society where we have access to purchasing wives from different countries and still call it love. What if love could be bought? Who would set the criteria for it? What would be your going rate to buy your love? Would it depend on the buyer? When it came to marrying our wives, we didn't have to pay a deposit and, if it didn't go as planned, get a full refund in return. Instead, we invested our time, effort, and began forging a relationship with a woman that we envisioned spending the rest of our lives loving. Love isn't something you can just up and buy, but rather a daily effort on your behalf to continue to fall deeper in love, building trust and communicating. Love is such a precious thing in the sight of God; one scripture says, "God is love!" What better example could one have concerning love than God? See, God's love is never predicated on how good or how many lives we touch; his love is freely given. God's love is unconditional; is yours? Is your love able to be hurt and still love as if nothing ever happened? I don't know what you may be holding onto that prevents you from loving your wife unconditionally, but seek God and allow his love to become your love. Watch it water your marriage and begin to flourish.

Prayer: God, thank you for loving us when we couldn't love ourselves, when we didn't know how to love, but you stepped in and gave us a reason to express and show love. You have truly blessed us with women that we all hold and love dearly as our wives, but give us a love that has no boundaries, limitations, stipulations, walls, or barriers. Allow us to love our wives as you desire for us to and allow us to continue to seek your face in this daily process. We thank you in advance, in Jesus's name, Amen!

Day 26 of 30 Prayer for Wives

Thought: What direction is your marriage heading?

Scripture: "Can two people walk together without agreeing on the direction?" (Amos 3:3 NLT).

Which Way Are You Going?

As many of us have learned through our marriages, sometimes we don't see eye to eye on the how, what, when, and where of life all the time. I have learned that if you and your wife are truly able to make a decision as one, God will honor it in ways that you couldn't even imagine. I'm a firm believer in this because I've experienced it. The direction your marriage goes after these thirty days will be entirely up to you. Now it can move forward, or it could take a turn for the worse. My prayer is that it would begin to move forward to a place that you know God has led it. If we begin to apply the godly principles to our lives as husbands, they will find a way into our marriages. Ask yourself this: Am I willing to show more patience? Understanding? Compassion? Love? If the answer is "yes," then you, your wife, and your marriage are headed in the right direction. How can two walk together unless they agree?

Prayer: God, give us direction in our marriages to be able to lead our families with wisdom. Allow us to walk together as one with our wives so that we may bring you glory and that our marriages stay on course to fulfill our vow, always headed in the right direction. In Jesus's name, Amen!

Day 27 of 30 Prayer for Wives

Thought: What are you speaking into your wife's life?

Scripture: "The tongue can bring death or life; those who love to talk will reap the consequences" (Proverbs 18:21 NLT)

Weed and Feed

God has a unique way of allowing things to have a dual purpose in our lives. Anyone who has a yard has encountered the issue of weeds and the challenge of killing them without killing the grass. So they invented weed and feed. This product has the ability to kill what is detrimental to the grass but has the benefit of keeping and growing a healthier yard. My question to you is this: How much weed and feed are you using in your marriage? Or have you just been using weed killer to kill the things trying to produce a healthier marriage? Husbands, we have the ability to speak life or death over our marriages. We can kill the things that are harmful and feed the things that make our marriages healthier than they have ever been. But the choice is up to us. Don't you want to come home to a wife who knows in the depths of her soul that you are trying to grow with her? I'm a believer that if you sow good seeds, you should look for a good harvest. But if you sow seeds of discord and confusion, expect to reap a harvest full of it. Our love for our wives should be indescribable when they are asked about the way we love them. For you fathers who are husbands, think about the love you felt when you held your first child in your arms. What a feeling, right? It was probably hard to articulate how you felt at that moment. So why not give our wives that same feeling each and every day? They are more than deserving! So begin killing the harmful things by speaking death over them and speak life to your marriage so things can grow and benefit your wife as well as your marriage.

Prayer: God, we speak life to our marriage so that it may grow and become healthier than it has ever been. We speak death to the things that have negatively impacted our marriages. We ask that you would remove these barriers, obstacles, and distractions out of the way. Our desire is to love our wives in such a way that they can't articulate the way we make them feel because the love you have given us to bestow upon them is indescribable. We thank you and bless you in Jesus's name, Amen!

Day 28 of 30 Prayer for Wives

Thought: If you were to rate your marriage solely based on you as a husband, what would it be? (Scale 1–10, 1: worst, 10: best.)

Scripture: "Make every effort to keep yourselves united in the Spirit, binding yourselves together with peace" (Ephesians 4:3 NLT).

Welcome to Ministry

How often do you pray for your wife? Marriage? Yourself? Do you exhaust every resource to keep peace? As husbands, we sometimes are more compassionate and understanding to the outside world than we are to our own household. How many times have you heard your wife say, "You care more about that than you do me?" Those words are tough to hear, especially when you feel that you are doing the best you can.

The reality of the situation is that we (husbands) have people who depend on us just as much as our own families, but our first ministry is our marriage. Paul says in the book of Corinthians, seventh chapter, "That he wished we all were single, but we each have our own gifts." Everyone doesn't desire the ministry of marriage, but you consciously decide to enter it. This ministry requires that you give and exhaust every avenue or resource possible to ensure that it grows, that it prospers, that it impacts those around you, inspires those in troubled situations in marriage, and those who believe that they can one day find love. Marriage is a *powerful ministry, and it is your ministry*! Do all that you can so your ministry doesn't die!

Prayer: God, thank you for the ministry of marriage. Some of us have just started, and others have been in it for quite some time now, but we ask that you allow this ministry to reach for the pinnacle of success to bring you glory. Help us in the coming days, weeks, months, and years to reach the full potential in our marriages as husbands to help others who are on this same journey. In Jesus's name, Amen!

Day 29 of 30 Prayer for Wives

Thought: No matter how good or bad your marriage may get, *never stop praying!*

Scripture: "Never stop praying. Be thankful in all circumstances, for this is God's will for you who belong to Christ Jesus" (1 Thessalonians 5:17–18 NLT).

Pray Without Ceasing!

As husbands, we have experienced some highs and lows in our marriages, but one thing I believe we all should find comfort in is prayer. Prayer shouldn't be a last-ditch effort to save a marriage or a plea to God to do something on your behalf but should always be the source you go to for direction, wisdom, and understanding. Will there be times when we don't know what to pray for? Yes, but that shouldn't stop you from thanking God in prayer for all the good things going on in your marriage, nor should it stop you from seeking God before things hit a rough patch. "In all things give thanks, for this is the will of God concerning you." Continue to pray for your wife even when you don't feel like it, when you are at your lowest, and even when things are the best they have ever been. Don't stop praying! Prayer will change you as a husband and improve your marriage.

Prayer: God, thank you for the ability to pray and for the women who mean the most to us in our lives. Continue to keep us focused on praying daily and keeping you first in our marriage. We trust that you will make us the husbands you desire us to be. In Jesus's name, Amen!

Day 30 of 30 Prayer for Wives

Thought: Would your wife find you guilty of being a good husband? A great husband? Or a godly husband?

Scripture: "Most important of all, continue to show deep love for each other, for love covers a multitude of sins" (1 Peter 4:8 NLT).

Found Guilty

Husbands, be found guilty of loving your wives, caring for them, listening to them, and supporting them. We have a lifelong journey with these beautiful women, and we can make the best of it, or we can allow it to become a terrible experience. The love you share with your wife daily allows it to grow and foster other areas of your marriage. Let your wife know that she is the most important person in your life. It's time for us as men to reflect on past experiences in marriage and learn from them. We know that marriage can be a very difficult thing at times, but would you trade it for anything in the world? We have the privilege to hold the title of husband, but we must not take it for granted or become complacent. Give your wife the best of you. I pray these last thirty days have helped and touched you in areas as a husband that need improving or solidified you are on the right track. Continue to be the great husband God has called for you to be.

Prayer: God, my prayer is for you to continue to watch over and bless husbands. You know what we all need to have success in our marriages and what we as men need to be greater and godly husbands. As we pursue a more intimate relationship with you, may it overflow into our marriages. Let your glory rest, rule, and reign in our marriages, homes, children, spiritual walk, and finances. Grow us to be the men you have predestined us to become for your glory. Bless us in our lifelong journeys and allow us to become blessings to those we come in contact with too. I ask these and all other blessings in your precious name, Jesus, Amen!

About the Author

Isaiah T. Hayes was born on April 5, 1985, to the late Millard "Joseph" Hayes Jr. and Rosie Hayes in Wiesbaden, Germany, on a United States Army base. Gazing into his little face, no one could have known he would grow up to be a cherished son, brother, husband to Ebony, father to Essence and Estelle, mentor, and friend to many.

In middle school, Isaiah shared his dream of becoming a pastor, a vision parents hope their children will pursue. And pursue it he did, guided by his faith. Living a life dedicated to God brings its share of challenges and joys, but to add "author" to his achievements is truly an honor. He may be the first to admit he's not perfect, but it's evident that he's a man of God with a heart of gold.

Words cannot convey the pride that his father would feel for his achievements. He has always been someone who listens and strives to resolve issues. He consistently makes an effort to recognize the good in everyone. In this book, you will discover that he has devoted time with God to help husbands comprehend the divine calling of marriage in relation to their wives.

www.ingramcontent.com/pod-product-compliance
Lightning Source LLC
Chambersburg PA
CBHW021134130726
47988CB00003B/1301